# ITALIAN

## *Made Nice & Easy!*™

**Staff of Research & Education Association**
**Carl Fuchs, Language Program Director**

**Based on Language Courses developed by the**
**U.S. Government for Foreign Service Personnel**

***Research & Education Association***
61 Ethel Road West
Piscataway, New Jersey 08854

**Dr. M. Fogiel, Director**

# ITALIAN MADE NICE & EASY™

Printed in the United States of America

Library of Congress Control Number 00-193027

International Standard Book Number 0-87891-371-8

# What This Guide Will Do For You

Whether travelling to a foreign country or to your favorite international restaurant, this *Nice & Easy* guide gives you just enough of the language to get around and be understood. Much of the material in this book was developed for government personnel who are often assigned to a foreign country on a moment's notice and need a quick introduction to the language.

In this handy and compact guide, you will find useful words and phrases, popular expressions, common greetings, and the words for numbers, money, and time. Every word or phrase is accompanied with the correct pronunciation and spelling. There is a vocabulary list for finding words quickly.

Generous margins on the pages allow you to make notes and remarks that you may find helpful.

If you expect to travel to Italy, the section on the country's history and relevant up-to-date facts will make your trip more informative and enjoyable. By keeping this guide with you, you'll be well prepared to understand as well as converse in Italian.

Carl Fuchs
Language Program Director

# Contents

# ITALY

# FACTS & HISTORY

**Official Name:** Republic of Italy

**Geography**
Area: 301,225 sq. km. (116,303 sq. mi.); about the size of Georgia and Florida combined.
Cities: *Capital*—Rome (pop. 2.7 million). *Other cities*—Milan, Naples, Turin.
Terrain: Mostly rugged and mountainous.
Climate: Generally mild Mediterranean; cold northern winters.

**People**
Nationality: *Noun and adjective*—Italian(s).
Population: 56.9 million.

Annual growth rate: 0.2%.

Ethnic groups: Primarily Italian, but there are small groups of German-, French-, Slovene-, and Albanian-Italians.

Religion: Roman Catholic (majority).

Language: Italian (official).

Education: *Years compulsory*—14. *Literacy*—98%.

Health: *Infant mortality rate*—8/1,000 live births. *Life expectancy*—74 yrs.

Work force (23 million): *Services*—61%.

# History of Italy

Italy is largely homogeneous linguistically and religiously but is diverse culturally, economically, and politically. Italy has the fifth highest population density in Europe—about 200 persons per square kilometer. Minority groups are small, the two largest being the German-speaking people of Bolzano Province and the Slovenes around Trieste. Other groups comprise small communities of Albanian, Greek, Ladino, and French origin. Although Roman Catholicism is the majority religion—99% of the people are nominally Catholic—all religious faiths are provided equal freedom before the law by the constitution.

Greeks settled in the southern tip of the Italian Peninsula in the eighth and seventh centuries B.C.; Etruscans, Romans, and others inhabited the central and northern mainland. The peninsula subsequently was unified under the Roman Republic. The neighboring islands also came under Roman control by the third century B.C. By the first century A.D., the Roman Empire effectively dominated the Mediterranean world. After the collapse of the Roman Empire in the west in the fifth century A.D., the peninsula and islands were subjected to a series of invasions, and political unity was lost. Italy became an oft-changing succession of small states, principalities, and kingdoms which fought among themselves and were subject to ambitions of foreign powers. Popes of Rome ruled central Italy; rivalries between the popes and the Holy Roman Emperors, who claimed Italy as their domain, often made the peninsula a battleground.

The commercial prosperity of northern and central Italian cities, beginning in the 11th century, and the influence of the Renaissance mitigated somewhat the effects of these medieval political rivalries. Although Italy declined after the 16th century, the Renaissance had strengthened the idea of a single Italian nationality. By the early 19th century, a nationalist movement developed and led to the reunification of Italy—except for Rome—in the 1860s. In 1861, Victor Emmanuel II of the House of Savoy was proclaimed King of Italy. Rome was incorporated in 1870. From 1870 until 1922, Italy was a constitutional monarchy with a parliament elected under limited suffrage.

During World War I, Italy renounced its standing alliance with Germany and Austria-Hungary and, in 1915, entered the war on the side of the Allies. Under the postwar settlement, Italy received some former Austrian territory along the northeast frontier. In 1922, Benito Mussolini came to power and, over the next few years, eliminated political parties, curtailed personal liberties, and installed a fascist dictatorship termed the Corporate State. The king, with little or no effective power, remained titular head of state.

Italy then allied with Germany and declared war

on the United Kingdom and France in 1940. In 1941, Italy—with the other Axis powers, Germany and Japan—declared war on the United States and the Soviet Union. Following the Allied invasion of Sicily in 1943, the King dismissed Mussolini and appointed Marshal Pietro Badoglio as premier. The Badoglio government declared war on Germany, which quickly occupied most of the country and freed Mussolini, who led a brief-lived regime in the north. An anti-fascist popular resistance movement grew during the last two years of the war, harassing German forces before they were driven out in April 1945. The monarchy was ended by a 1946 plebiscite, and a constituent assembly was elected to draw up plans for the republic.

Under the 1947 peace treaty, minor adjustments were made in Italy's frontier with France. The eastern border area was transferred to Yugoslavia, and the area around the city of Trieste was designated a free territory. In 1954, the free territory, which had remained under the administration of U.S.-U.K. forces (Zone A, including the city of Trieste) and Yugoslav forces (Zone B), was divided between Italy and Yugoslavia, principally along the zonal boundary. This arrangement was made permanent by the Italian-Yugoslav

Treaty of Osimo, ratified in 1977. Under the 1947 peace treaty, Italy also gave up its overseas territories and certain Mediterranean islands.

The Roman Catholic Church's status in Italy has been determined, since its temporal powers ended in 1870, by a series of accords with the Italian government. Under the Lateran Pacts of 1929, which were confirmed by the present constitution, the state of Vatican City is recognized by Italy as an independent, sovereign entity. While preserving that recognition, in 1984, Italy and the Vatican updated several provisions of the 1929 accords. Included was the end of Roman Catholicism as Italy's formal state religion.

# Italy's Cultural Contributions

Europe's Renaissance period began in Italy during the 14th and 15th centuries. Literary achievements—such as the poetry of Petrarch, Tasso, and Ariosto and the prose of Boccaccio, Machiavelli, and Castiglione—exerted a tremendous and lasting influence on the subsequent development of Western civilization, as did the painting, sculpture, and architecture contributed by giants such as Leonardo da Vinci, Raphael, Botticelli, Fra Angelico, and Michelangelo.

The musical influence of Italian composers Monteverdi, Palestrina, and Vivaldi proved epochal; in the 19th century, Italian romantic opera flourished under composers Gioacchino Rossini, Giuseppe Verdi, and Giacomo Puccini. Contemporary Italian artists, writers, filmmakers, architects, composers, and designers contribute significantly to Western culture.

# Government & Politics

Italy has been a democratic republic since June 2, 1946, when the monarchy was abolished by popular referendum. The constitution was promulgated on January 1, 1948.

The Italian state is highly centralized. The prefect of each of the provinces is appointed by and answerable to the central government. In addition to the provinces, the constitution provides for 20 regions with limited governing powers. Five regions—Sardinia, Sicily, Trentino-Alto Adige, Valle d'Aosta, and Friuli-Venezia Giulia—function with special autonomy statutes. The other 15 regions were established in 1970 and vote for regional "councils." The establishment of regional governments throughout Italy has brought some decentralization to the national governmental machinery.

The 1948 constitution established a bicameral Parliament (Chamber of Deputies and Senate), a separate judiciary, and an executive branch composed of a Council of Ministers (cabinet) which is headed by the president of the council (prime minister). The president of the republic is elected for seven years by the Parliament sitting jointly with a small number of regional delegates. The president nominates the prime minister, who chooses the other ministers.

**Trevi fountain, Rome**

Campania, Positano

**Vittorio Emmanuel Monument, Rome**

## Hints on Pronunciation

You will find all the words and phrases written both in Italian spelling and in a simplified spelling which you read like English. Don't use the Italian spelling, the one given in parentheses, unless you have studied Italian before. *Read the simplified spelling as though it were English.* When you see the Italian word for "excuse me" spelled *SKOO-za*, give the *oo* the sound it has in the English words *too*, *boot*, etc. and not the sound it has in German or any other language you may happen to know.

Each letter or combination of letters is used for the sound it usually stands for in English and it *always*

**3**

stands for that sound. Thus, *oo* is always pronounced as it is in *boo, too, boot, tooth, roost*, never as anything else. Say these words and then pronounce the vowel sound by itself. That is the sound you must use every time you see *oo* in the *Pronunciation* column. If you should use some other sound—for example, the sound of *oo* in *blood*—you might be misunderstood.

Syllables that are accented, that is, pronounced louder than others, are written in capital letters. In Italian unaccented syllables are not skipped over quickly, as they are in English. Hyphens are used to divide words into syllables in order to make them easier to pronounce. Curved lines (‿) are used to show sounds that are pronounced together without any break; for example, *beek-K‿YAY-ray* meaning "glass," *D‿YAY-chee* meaning "ten."

## Special Points

| | |
|---|---|
| **AY** | as in *may, say, play* but don't drawl it the way we do in English. Since it is not drawled it sounds almost like the *e* in *let*. Example: *do-VAY* meaning "where is?" |
| **O** *or* **OH** | as in *go, so, oh, note, joke* but don't drawl it the way we do in English. Since it is not drawled it sounds somewhat like the *aw* in *law*. Example: *NO* meaning "no." |

4

**Leaning Tower of Pisa**

**Casa de Fauna, Pompeii**

Major Church of San Giorgia, Venice

## GREETINGS AND GENERAL PHRASES

| *English* | *Pronunciation and Italian Spelling* |
|---|---|
| **Good morning** *or* **Good day** | *bwohn JOR-no*   (Buon giorno) |
| **Good evening** | *BWO-na SAY-ra*   (Buona sera) |
| **Sir** *or* **Mister** | *seen-YO-ray*   (signore) |
| **Madam** | *seen-YO-ra*   (signora) |
| **Miss** | *seen-yo-REE-na*   (signorina) |

Italians have two phrases for "please" which they use very often. They are:

| **Please** | *payr p̄_ya-CHAY-ray*   (per piacere) |
|---|---|
| *or* | *payr fa-VO-ray*   (per favore) |
| **Excuse me** | *SKOO-za*   (scusa) |

| English | Pronunciation and Italian Spelling |
|---------|-----------------------------------|
| Thank you | *GRAHTS-yay* (grazie) |
| Yes | *SEE* (sì) |
| No | *NO* (no) |
| Do you understand? | *ah-VAY-tay ka-PEE-to?* (Avete capito?) |
| I don't understand | *NOHN ka-PEE-sko* (Non capisco) |
| Speak slowly | *par-LA-tay ah-DA-jo* (Parlate adagio) |

### LOCATION

When you need directions to get somewhere you use the phrase "where is" and then add the words you need.

| | |
|---|---|
| Where is | *[DO-vay AY] do VAY* ([Dove è] Dov'è) |
| the restaurant? | *eel ress-to-RAHN* (il restaurant) |
| Where is the restaurant? | *[DO-vay AY] do-VAY eel ress-to-RAHN?* ([Dove è] Dov'è il restaurant?) |
| hotel | *o-TEL* (hotel) |
| or | *ahl-BAYR-go* (albergo) |
| Where is a hotel? | *[DO-vay AY] do-VAY lo-TEL?* ([Dove è] Dov'è l'hotel?) |
| or | *[DO-vay AY] do-VAY lahl-BAYR-go?* ([Dove è] Dov'è l'albergo?) |
| the railroad station | *la stahts-YO-nay* (la stazione) |

| English | Pronunciation and Italian Spelling |
|---|---|
| Where is the railroad station? | [*DO-vay A Y*] *do-VA Y la stahts-YO-nay?* ([Dove è] Dov'è la stazione?) |
| a toilet | *eel ga-bee-NET-to*   il gabinetto |
| Where is a toilet? | [*DO-vay-A Y*] *do-VA Y eel ga-bee-NET-to?* ([Dove è] Dov'è il gabinetto?) |

### DIRECTIONS

The answer to your question "Where is such and such" may be "Turn right," or "Turn left" or "Straight ahead," so you need to know these phrases:

| | | |
|---|---|---|
| **Turn right** | *JEE-ra ah DESS-tra* | (Gira a destra) |
| **Turn left** | *JEE-ra ah see-NEE-stra* | (Gira a sinistra) |
| **Straight ahead** | *SEM-pray dee-REET-to* | (Sempre diritto) |

Paestum

It is sometimes useful to say "Please point."

**Please point**        *een-dee-KA-tay-mee, payr fa-VO-ray*
                        (Indicatemi, per favore)

If you are driving and ask the distance to another town it will be given to you in kilometers, not miles.

**Kilometers**          *kee-LO-may-tree*        chilometri

One kilometer equals ⅝ of a mile.

### NUMBERS

You need to know the numbers.

| English | Pronunciation | Italian |
|---------|---------------|---------|
| **One** | *OO-no* | uno |
| **Two** | *DOO-ay* | due |
| **Three** | *TRAY* | tre |
| Four | *KWAHT-tro* | quattro |
| **Five** | *CHEEN-kway* | cinque |
| Six | *SAY* | sei |
| **Seven** | *SET-tay* | sette |
| **Eight** | *OHT-to* | otto |
| **Nine** | *NO-vay* | nove |
| **Ten** | *D‿YAY-chee* | dieci |
| **Eleven** | *OON-dee-chee* | undici |

| English | Pronunciation and Italian Spelling | |
|---|---|---|
| Twelve | *DO-dee-chee* | dodici |
| Thirteen | *TRAY-dee-chee* | tredici |
| Fourteen | *kwaht-TOR-dee-chee* | quattordici |
| Fifteen | *KWEEN-dee-chee* | quindici |
| Sixteen | *SAY-dee-chee* | sedici |
| Seventeen | *dee-chahss-SET-tay* | diciassette |
| Eighteen | *dee-CHOHT-to* | diciotto |
| Nineteen | *dee-chahn-NO-vay* | diciannove |
| Twenty | *VEN-tee* | venti |
| Twenty-one | *ven-TOO-no* | ventuno |
| Twenty-two | *ven-tee-DOO-ay* | ventidue (and so forth) |
| Thirty | *TREN-ta* | trenta |
| Thirty-one | *tren-TOO-no* | trentuno |
| Thirty-two | *tren-ta-DOO-ay* | trentadue (and so forth) |
| Forty | *kwa-RAHN-ta* | quaranta |
| Fifty | *cheen-KWAHN-ta* | cinquanta |
| Sixty | *sess-SAHN-ta* | sessanta |
| Seventy | *set-TAHN-ta* | settanta |

| English | Pronunciation and Italian Spelling | |
|---------|-----------------|---------|
| Eighty | *oht-TAHN-ta* | ottanta |
| Ninety | *no-VAHN-ta* | novanta |
| Hundred | *CHEN-to* | cento |
| Thousand | *MEEL-lay* | mille |

## WHAT'S THIS?

When you want to know the name of something you can say "What's this?" and point to the thing you mean.

| | | |
|---------|-----------------|---------|
| What is | *[KO-za AY] ko-ZAY* | ([Cosa è] Cos'è) |
| this | *KWESS-to* | (questo) |
| What's this? | *[KO-za AY] ko-ZAY KWESS-to?* | |
| | ([Cosa è] Cos'è questo?) | |

## ASKING FOR THINGS

When you want something, you can say "I want" and add the name of the thing wanted.

| | | |
|---------|-----------------|---------|
| I want | *EE͜o day-ZEE-day-ro* | (Io desidero) |
| *or* | *EE͜o VOHL-yo* | (Io voglio) |
| cigarettes | *see-ga-RET-tay* | (sigarette) |
| I want cigarettes | *EE͜o day-ZEE-day-ro see-ga-RET-tay* | |
| | (Io desidero sigarette) | |
| to eat | *mahn-JA-ray* | (mangiare) |
| I want to eat | *EE͜o day-ZEE-day-ro mahn-JA-ray* | |
| | (Io desidero mangiare) | |

10

Piazza Navona, Rome

**Santa Maria Del Fiore Cathedral, Florence**

| English | Pronunciation and Italian Spelling |
|---------|-----------------------------------|

Here are the words for some of the things you may require:

| English | Pronunciation and Italian Spelling |
|---------|-----------------------------------|
| bread | *PA-nay*  (pane) |
| butter | *BOOR-ro*  (burro) |
| soup | *mee-NESS-tra*  (minestra) |
| fish | *PAY-shay*  (pesce) |
| meat | *KAR-nay*  (carne) |
| steak | *bee-STEK-ka*  (bistecca) |
| lamb | *ahn-YEL-lo*  (agnello) |
| veal | *vee-TEL-lo*  (vitello) |
| pork | *ma-YA-lay*  (maiale) |
| beef | *MAHN-dzo*  (manzo) |
| chicken | *POHL-lo*  (pollo) |
| eggs | *WO-va*  (uova) |
| fruit | *FROOT-ta*  (frutta) |
| vegetables | *vayr-DOO-ra*  (verdura) |
| or | *lay-GOO-mee*  (legumi) |
| potatoes | *pa-TA-tay*  (patate) |
| beans | *fa-JO-lee*  (fagioli) |
| sugar | *TSOOK-kay-ro*  (zucchero) |

| English | Pronunciation and Italian Spelling |
|---|---|
| salt | *SA-lay*  (sale) |
| pepper | *PAY-pay*  (pepe) |
| rice | *REE-zo*  (riso) |
| salad | *een-sa-LA-ta*  (insalata) |
| tomato | *po-mo-DO-ro*  (pomodoro) |
| orange | *ah-RAHN-cha*  (arancia) |
| lemon | *lee-MO-nay*  (limone) |
| milk | *LAHT-tay*  (latte) |
| ice cream | *jay-LA-to*  (gelato) |
| chocolate | *chohk-ko-LA-ta*  (cioccolata) |
| tobacco | *ta-BAHK-ko*  (tabacco) |
| drinking water | *AHK-kwa po-TA-bee-lay*  (acqua potabile) |
| cup of tea | *TAHT-tsa dee TAY*  (tazza di tè) |
| cup of coffee | *TAHT-tsa dee kahf-FAY*  (tazza di caffè) |
| glass of beer | *beek-K⏝YAY-ray dee BEER-ra*  (bicchiere di birra) |
| bottle of wine | *F⏝YA-sko dee VEE-no*  (fiasco di vino) |
| matches | *f⏝yahm-MEE-fay-ree*  (fiammiferi) |

## MONEY

To find out how much things cost you say "How much costs?"

| How much | *KWAHN-to* | Quanto |
| costs | *KO-sta* | costa |
| How much does this cost? | *KWAHN-to KO-sta?* | Quanto costa? |

## TIME

To find out what time it is you say "What hour is it?"

**What time is it?** *kay O-ra AY?*    (Che ora è?)

For "Two o'clock" you say "They are the two."

**Two o'clock**    *SO-no lay DOO-ay*    (sono le due)

"Ten past two" is "The two and ten."

**Ten past two**    *lay DOO-ay ay D_YAY-chee*
(le due e dieci)

"Quarter past five" is "The five and a quarter."

**Quarter past five**    *lay CHEEN-kway ay oon KWAHR-to*
(le cinque e un quarto)

"Half past six" is "The six and a half."

**Half past six**    *lay SAY ay MED-dza*    (le sei e mezza)

**13**

"Quarter of eight" is "The eight minus a quarter."

| **Quarter of eight** | *lay OHT-to MAY-no oon KWAR-to* (le otto meno un quarto) |

You may also say:

*oon KWAR-to AHL-lay OHT-to*
(un quarto alle otto)

"Three minutes to nine" is "The nine minus three."

**Three minutes to nine**   *lay NO-vay MAY-no TRAY*
(le nove meno tre)

If you want to know when a movie starts or when the train leaves you say:

**At what hour**      *ah KAY O-ra*   (A che ora)

**begins**            *ko-MEEN-cha*   (comincia)

**the film**          *eel FEELM*   (il film)

**When does the movie start?**   *ah KAY O-ra ko-MEEN-cha eel FEELM?*
(A che ora comincia il film?)

**the train**         *eel TRAY-no*   (il treno)

**leaves**            *PAR-tay*   (parte)

**When does the train leave?**   *ah KAY·O-ra PAR-tay eel TRAY-no?*
(A che ora parte il treno?)

**Yesterday**         *YAY-ree*   (ieri)

| English | Pronunciation and Italian Spelling |
|---------|-----------------------------------|
| Today | *OHD-jee* (oggi) |
| Tomorrow | *do-MA-nee* (domani) |

The days of the week are:

| Sunday | *do-MAY-nee-ka* (domenica) |
|--------|---------------------------|
| Monday | *loo-nay-DEE* (lunedì) |
| Tuesday | *mar-tay-DEE* (martedì) |
| Wednesday | *mayr-ko-lay-DEE* (mercoledì) |
| Thursday | *jo-vay-DEE* (giovedì) |
| Friday | *vay-nayr-DEE* (venerdì) |
| Saturday | *SA-ba-to* (sabato) |

## USEFUL PHRASES

The following phrases will be useful:

| What is your name? | *KO-may see K͜YA-ma?* (Come si chiama?) |
|--------------------|----------------------------------------|
| My name is___ | *EE͜o mee K͜YA-mo___* (Io mi chiamo___) |
| How do you say *table* (or anything else) in Italian? | *KO-may see K͜YA-ma* table *een ee-tahl-YA-no?* (Come si chiama *table* in italiano?) |
| Good-by | *ar-ree-vay-DAYR-chee* (Arrivederci) |

**15**

### ADDITIONS AND NOTES

Another way to say restaurant is:

> *eel ree-sto-RAHN-tay*   (il ristorante)

A *F⌣YA-sko* is a bottle containing 2 liters, equal to about half a gallon. In Italy wine is generally sold in bottles of this size.

Another common way to say the sentence "How do you say *table* in Italian?" is:

> *KO-may see DEE-chay* table *een ee-tahl-YA-no?*   (Come si dice *table* in italiano?)

**Montepulciano**

Castle of Cornedo

Vallombrosa, Tuscany

Gondola tour, Venice

## ADDITIONAL EXPRESSIONS

| *English* | *Pronunciation and Italian Spelling* |
|-----------|--------------------------------------|
| I am hungry | *O FA-may*  (Ho fame) |
| I am thirsty | *O SAY-tay*  (Ho sete) |
| I am well | *STO BAY-nay*  (Sto bene) |
| Stop! | *fayr-MA-tay-vee!*  (Fermatevi!) |
| Come here! | *vay-NEE-tay KWEE!*  (Venite quì!) |
| Right away *or* Quickly | *PRESS-to*  (Presto) |
| Come quickly! | *vay-NEE-tay PRESS-to!*  (Venite presto!) |
| Go quickly! | *ahn-DA-tay PRESS-to!*  (Andate presto!) |
| Help! | *ah-YOO-to!*  (Aiuto!) |
| Help me | *ah-yoo-TA-tay-mee*  (Aiutatemi) |
| Bring help | *k⌣ya-MA-tay day sohk-KOR-see*  (Chiamate dei soccorsi) |
| I will pay you | *VEE pa-gay-RO*  (Vi pagherò) |
| Where is the town? | *do-VAY eel pa-AY-zay?*  (Dov'è il paese?) |

**17**

| English | Pronunciation and Italian Spelling |
|---|---|
| Where is it? | *do-VA Y?* (Dov'è?) |
| How far is the town? | *ah KA Y deess-TA HN-tsa A Y eel pa-A Y-zay?* (A che distanza è il paese?) |
| Is it far? | *A Y lohn-TA-no?* (È lontano?) |
| How far is it? | *ah KA Y dee-STA HN-tsa A Y?* (A che distanza è?) |
| Which way is north? | *do-VA Y eel NORD?* (Dov'è il nord?) |
| Which is the road to___? | *kwa-LA Y la STRA-da payr___?* (Qual'è la strada per___?) |
| Draw me a map | *FA-tay-mee oo-no SKEET-tso* (Fatemi uno schizzo) |
| Take me there | *ahk-kohm-pahn-YA-tay-mee LA* (Accompagnatemi là) |
| Take me to a doctor | *ahk-kohm-pahn-YA-tay-mee da oon MA Y-dee-ko* (Accompagnatemi da un medico) |
| Take me to the hospital | *ahk-kohm-pahn-YA-tay-mee ahl-lo-spay-DA-lay* (Accompagnatemi all'ospedale) |
| Danger! | *pay-REE-ko-lo!* (Pericolo!) |
| Watch out! | *aht-tents-YO-nay!* (Attenzione!) |
| Gas! | *GAHSS!* (Gas!) |
| Take cover! | *MET-tayr-see ahl ree-PA-ro!* (Mettersi al riparo!) |
| Wait a minute! | *ah-spet-TA-tay oon mee-NOO-to!* (Aspettate un minuto!) |
| Good luck | *BWO-na for-TOO-na* (Buona fortuna) |

**Park D'Alassio Fountain, Riviera**

**Duomo Cathedral, Milan**

# FILL-IN SENTENCES

In this section you will find a number of sentences, each containing a blank space which can be filled in with any one of the words in the list that follows. For example, in order to say "Where can I get some soap?" look for the phrase "Where can I get____?" in the English column and find the Italian expression given beside it; in this case it is *DO-vay POHSS-so tro-VA-ray____*. Then look for "soap" in the list that follows; the Italian is *del sa-PO-nay*. Put the word for "soap" in the blank space and you get *DO-vay POHSS-so tro-VA-ray del sa-PO-nay?*

| English | Pronunciation and Italian Spelling |
|---|---|
| I want____ | *day-ZEE-day-ro____* (Desidero____) |
| We want____ | *day-zee-dayr-YA-mo____* (Desideriamo____) |
| Give me____ | *DA-tay-mee____* (Datemi____) |
| Bring me____ | *por-TA-tay-mee____* (Portatemi____) |
| Where can I get____? | *DO-vay POHSS-so tro-VA-ray____?* (Dove posso trovare____?) |
| I have____ | *O____* (Ho____) |
| We have____ | *ahb-B⌣YA-mo____* (Abbiamo____) |
| I don't have____ | *nohn O____* (Non ho____) |
| We don't have____ | *nohn ahb-B⌣YA-mo____* (Non abbiamo____) |
| Have you____? | *ah-VAY-tay____?* (Avete____?) |

| English | Pronunciation and Italian Spelling |
|---------|-----------------------------------|

**EXAMPLE**

| | |
|---|---|
| **I want___** | *day-ZEE-day-ro___*   (Desidero___) |
| **food** | *da mahn-JA-ray*   (da mangiare) |
| **I want food** | *day-ZEE-day-ro da mahn-JA-ray* (Desidero da mangiare) |

| | |
|---|---|
| **food** | *da mahn-JA-ray*   (da mangiare) |
| **apples** | *MAY-lay*   (mele) |
| **boiled water** | *del-LAHK-kwa bohl-LEE-ta*   (dell'acqua bollita) |
| **carrots** | *ka-RO-tay*   (carote) |
| **cucumbers** | *chee-tree-O-lee*   (citrioli) |
| **grapes** | *OO-va*   (uva) |
| **ham** | *pro-SHOOT-to*   (prosciutto) |
| **onions** | *chee-POHL-lay*   (cipolle) |
| **peas** | *pee-ZEL-lee*   (piselli) |
| **spinach** | *spee-NA-chee*   (spinaci) |
| **turnips** | *RA-pay*   (rape) |
| *(for other foods see page 10)* | |
| **a cup** | *oo-na TAHT-tsa*   (una tazza) |
| **a fork** | *oo-na for-KET-ta*   (una forchetta) |

| English | Pronunciation and Italian Spelling |
|---------|-----------------------------------|
| a glass | *oon beek-K͜YAY-ray* (un bicchiere) |
| a knife | *oon kohl-TEL-lo* (un coltello) |
| a plate | *oon P͜YAHT-to* (un piatto) |
| a spoon | *oon kook-K͜YA-yo* (un cucchiaio) |
| | |
| a bed | *oon LET-to* (un letto) |
| blankets | *del-lay ko-PAYR-tay* (delle coperte) |
| a mattress | *oon ma-tay-RAHSS-so* (un materasso) |
| a pillow | *oon koo-SHEE-no* (un cuscino) |
| a room | *oo-na KA-may-ra* (una camera) |
| sheets | *del-lay lent-SWO-la* (delle lenzuola) |
| a towel | *oon ah-shoo-ga-MA-no* (un'asciugamano) |
| cigars | *DAY SEE-ga-ree* (dei sigari) |
| a pipe | *oo-na PEE-pa* (una pipa) |
| tobacco | *del ta-BAHK-ko* (del tabacco) |
| pipe tobacco | *ta-BAHK-ko payr PEE-pa* (tabacco per pipa) |
| | |
| a pen | *oo-na PEN-na* (una penna) |
| a pencil | *oo-na ma-TEE-ta* (una matita) |
| ink | *del-leenk-YOHS-tro* (dell'inchiostro) |

**21**

| English | Pronunciation and Italian Spelling |
|---------|-----------------------------------|
| a comb | *oon PET-tee-nay*  (un pettine) |
| hot water | *del-LAHK-kwa KAHL-da*  (dell'acqua calda) |
| a razor | *oon ra-ZO-yo*  (un rasoio) |
| razor blades | *del-lay LA-may da ra-ZO-yo*  (delle lame da rasoio) |
| a shaving brush | *oon pen-NEL-lo payr BAR-ba*  (un pennello per barba) |
| shaving soap | *del sa-PO-nay payr BAR-ba*  (del sapone per barba) |
| soap | *del sa-PO-nay*  (del sapone) |
| a tooth- brush | *oo-no spat-tso-LEE-no da DEN-tee*  (uno spazzolino da denti) |
| tooth paste | *del-la PA-sta den-tee-FREE-cha*  (della pasta dentifricia) |
| tooth powder | *pohl-VAY-ray den-tee-FREE-cha*  (polvere dentifricia) |
| a handker- chief | *oon faht-tso-LET-to*  (un fazzoletto) |
| a raincoat | *oon eem-payr-may-AH-bee-lay*  (un impermeabile) |
| a shirt | *oo-na ka-MEE-cha*  (una camicia) |

| English | Pronunciation and Italian Spelling |
|---------|-----------------------------------|
| shoe laces | *day LAHT-chee da SKAR-pay* (dei lacci da scarpe) |
| shoe polish | *del-la CHAY-ra payr SKAR-pay* (della cera per scarpe) |
| shoes | *del-lay SKAR-pay* (delle scarpe) |
| undershirt | *oo-na MAHL-ya* (una maglia) |
| under-shorts | *del-lay moo-TAHN-day* (delle mutande) |
| a needle | *oon AH-go* (un ago) |
| buttons | *day boht-TO-nee* (dei bottoni) |
| safety pins | *dayl-yee SPEEL-lee dee see-koo-RET-tsa* (degli spilli di sicurezza) |
| thread | *del FEE-lo da koo-CHEE-ray* (del filo da cucire) |
| adhesive tape | *chay-ROHT-to* (cerotto) |
| aspirin | *del-la-spee-REE-na* (dell'aspirina) |
| a bandage | *oo-na BEN-da* (una benda) |
| cotton | *del ko-TO-nay* (del cotone) |
| a disin-fectant | *oon dee-zeen-fet-TAHN-tay* (un disinfettante) |
| iodine | *teen-TOO-ra DOHD-yo* (tintura d'odio) |
| a laxative | *oon lahss-sa-TEE-vo* (un lassativo) |

**23**

| English | Pronunciation and Italian Spelling |
|---------|-----------------------------------|

**EXAMPLE**

| | |
|---|---|
| **I want to___** | *day-ZEE-day-ro___* (Desidero___) |
| **eat** | *mahn-JA-ray* (mangiare) |
| **I want to eat** | *day-ZEE-day-ro mahn-JA-ray* (Desidero mangiare) |

| | |
|---|---|
| **eat** | *mahn-JA-ray* (mangiare) |
| **drink** | *BAY-ray* (bere) |
| **wash up** | *la-VAR-mee* (lavarmi) |
| **take a bath** | *PREN-day-ray oon BAHN-yo* (prendere un bagno) |
| **rest** | *ree-po-ZA-ray* (riposare) |
| **sleep** | *dor-MEE-ray* (dormire) |
| **have my hair cut** | *FAR-mee tahl-YA-ray ee ka-PEL-lee* (farmi tagliare i capelli) |
| **be shaved** | *FAR-mee la BAR-ba* (farmi la barba) |
| **have my clothes washed** | *FAR la-VA-ray DEL-la b_yahn-kay-REE-ah* (far lavare della biancheria) |

A simple way of asking for a haircut in Italian is to use the word for "hair," which is *ka-PEL-lee*. When you want a shave, you can use the word for "beard," *BAR-ba*.

___

| English | Pronunciation and Italian Spelling |
|---------|-----------------------------------|
| Where is there___? | *DO-vay CHAY___?* (Dove c'è___?) |
| Where can I find___? | *DO-vay POHSS-so tro-VA-ray___?* (Dove posso trovare___?) |

**EXAMPLE**

| | |
|---------|-----------------------------------|
| Where is there___? | *DO-vay CHAY___?* (Dove c'è___?) |
| a barber | *oon barb-YAY-ray* (un barbiere) |
| Where is there a barber? | *DO-vay CHAY oon barb-YAY-ray?* (Dove c'è un barbiere?) |

| | | |
|---------|-------------|---------------------|
| a barber | *oon barb-YAY-ray* | (un barbiere) |
| a dentist | *oon den-TEE-sta* | (un dentista) |
| a doctor | *oon MAY-dee-ko* | (un medico) |
| a mechanic | *oon mek-KA-nee-ko* | (un meccanico) |
| a policeman | *oo-na GWARD-ya* | (una guardia) |
| a porter | *oon fahk-KEE-no* | (un facchino) |
| a servant | *oon ka-mayr-YAY-ray* | (un cameriere) |
| a shoe-maker | *oon kahl-tso-LA-yo* | (un calzolaio) |
| a tailor | *oon SAR-to* | (un sarto) |
| a workman | *oon o-pay-RA-yo* | (un operaio) |

**25**

| English | Pronunciation and Italian Spelling |
|---------|-----------------------------------|
| a church | *oo-na K͜YAY-za*   (una chiesa) |
| a clothing store | *oon nay-GOHTS-yo dee ar-TEE-ko-lee da WO-mo*   (un negozio di articoli da uomo) |
| a drugstore | *oo-na far-ma-CHEE-ah*   (una farmacia) |
| a garage | *oon ga-RAJ*   (un garage) |
| a grocery | *oon nay-GOHTS-yo dee JAY-nay-ree ah-lee-men-TA-ree*   (un negozio di generi alimentari) |
| a house | *oo-na KA-za*   (una casa) |
| a spring | *oo-na sor-JEN-tay*   (una sorgente) |
| a well | *oon POHT-tso*   (un pozzo) |

---

| Where is___? | *do-VAY___?*   (Dov'è___?) |
|---------|-----------------------------------|

**EXAMPLE**

| Where is___? | *do-VAY___?*   (Dov'è___?) |
|---------|-----------------------------------|
| the bridge | *eel POHN-tay*   (il ponte) |
| Where is the bridge? | *do-VAY eel POHN-tay?*   (Dov'è il ponte?) |

| the bridge | *eel POHN-tay*   (il ponte) |
|---------|-----------------------------------|
| the bus | *LA͜oo-to-booss*   (l'autobus) |

| English | Pronunciation and Italian Spelling |
|---------|-----------------------------------|
| the camp | *eel KAHM-po* (il campo) |
| the city | *la cheet-TA* (la città) |
| the highway | *la͜oo-to-STRA-da* (l'autostrada) |
| the hospital | *lo-spay-DA-lay* (l'ospedale) |
| the main street | *la STRA-da preen-chee-PA-lay* (la strada principale) |
| the market | *eel mayr-KA-to* (il mercato) |
| the nearest town | *eel pa-AY-zay P͜YOO vee-CHEE-no* (il paese più vicino) |
| the police station | *la kwess-TOO-ra* (la questura) |
| the post office | *loof-FEE-cho po-STA-lay* (l'ufficio postale) |
| the railroad | *la fayr-ro-VEE-ah* (la ferrovia) |
| the river | *eel F͜YOO-may* (il fiume) |
| the road | *la STRA-da* (la strada) |
| the telegraph office | *loof-FEE-cho tay-lay-GRA-fee-ko* (l'ufficio telegrafico) |
| the telephone | *eel tay-LAY-fo-no* (il telefono) |
| the town | *eel pa-AY-zay* (il paese) |

| English | Pronunciation and Italian Spelling |
|---------|-----------------------------------|
| I am___ | *SO-no___*  (Sono___) |
| He is___ | *EL-yee A Y___*  (Egli è___) |

**EXAMPLE**

| | |
|---------|-----------------------------------|
| I am___ | *SO-no___*  (Sono___) |
| an American | *ah-may-ree-KA-no*  (americano) |
| I am an American | *SO-no ah-may-ree-KA-no*  (Sono americano) |
| an American | *ah-may-ree-KA-no*  (americano) |
| sick | *ahm-ma-LA-to*  (ammalato) |
| wounded | *fay-REE-to*  (ferito) |
| lost | *spayr-DOO-to*  (sperduto) |
| tired | *STAHN-ko*  (stanco) |

---

| | |
|---------|-----------------------------------|
| We are___ | *S‿YA-mo___*  (Siamo___) |
| They are___ | *ESS-see SO-no___*  (Essi sono___) |
| Are you___? | *S‿YA Y-tay___?*  (Siete___?) |

**EXAMPLE**

| | |
|---------|-----------------------------------|
| We are___ | *S‿YA-mo___*  (Siamo___) |
| Americans | *ah-may-ree-KA-nee*  (americani) |
| We are Americans | *S‿YA-mo ah-may-ree-KA-nee*  (Siamo americani) |

Scaliger's Castle. Sirmione

| English | Pronunciation and Italian Spelling |
|---------|-----------------------------------|
| Americans | *ah-may-ree-KA-nee* (americani) |
| sick | *ahm-ma-LA-tee* (ammalati) |
| wounded | *fay-REE-tee* (feriti) |
| lost | *spayr-DOO-tee* (sperduti) |
| tired | *STAHN-kee* (stanchi) |

| | |
|---|---|
| It is___ | *A Y___* (È___) |
| Is it___? | *A Y___?* (È___?) |
| It is not___ | *nohn A Y___* (Non è___) |

**29**

| English | Pronunciation and Italian Spelling |
| --- | --- |
| | **EXAMPLE** |
| It is not___ | *nohn AY___*   (Non è___) |
| good | *BWO-no*  (buono) |
| It is not good | *nohn AY BWO-no*   (Non è buono) |
| | |
| good | *BWO-no*  (buono) |
| bad | *kaht-TEE-vo*  (cattivo) |
| expensive | *KA-ro*  (caro) |
| too expen-sive | *TROHP-po KA-ro*   (troppo caro) |
| here | *KWEE*  (quì) |
| there | *LA*  (là) |
| near | *vee-CHEE-no*  (vicino) |
| far | *lohn-TA-no*  (lontano) |

# IMPORTANT SIGNS

| *Italian* | *English* |
|---|---|
| Alt! | Stop! |
| Rallentare! | Go Slow! |
| Pericolo! | Danger! |
| Senso unico | One Way |
| Senso vietato | No Thoroughfare |
| Tenere la destra | Keep to the Right |
| Strada in costruzione | Road under Construction |
| Curva pericolosa | Dangerous Curve |
| A 300 metri arresto | Stop at 300 Meters |
| Attenti ai treni | Look Out for Locomotive |
| Pericolo di morte | High Tension Lines (Danger of death) |
| Incrocio pericoloso | Dangerous Crossing |
| Passaggio a livello | Grade Crossing |
| Divieto di parcheggio | No Parking |
| Vietato l'ingresso | No Admittance |
| Donne *or* Signore | Women |
| Uomini *or* Signori | Men |
| Vietato fumare | No Smoking |
| Vietato sputare | No Spitting |
| Entrata | Entrance |
| Uscita | Exit |

Mantua, Lombardy

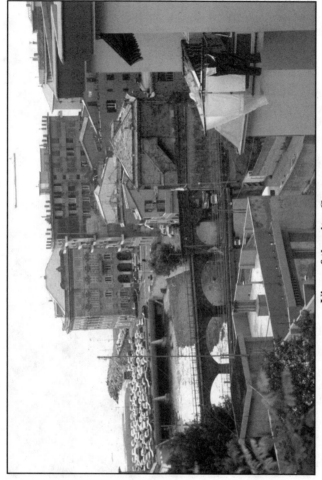

View of the city, Genoa

**Colosseum, Rome**

Old fortifications, Umbria, Assisi

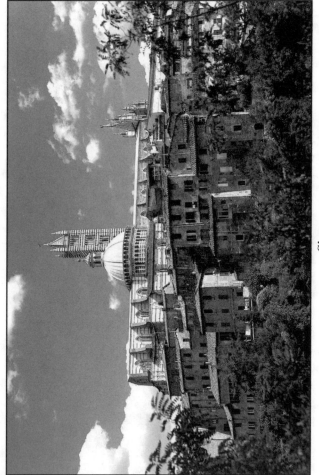

Siena

# ALPHABETICAL
# WORD LIST

| *English* | *Pronunciation and Italian Spelling* |
|---|---|
| | **A** |
| a | *oon*   (un) |
|     *or* | *oo-na*   (una) |
| adhesive tape | *chay-ROHT-to*   (cerotto) |
| am | |
|   I am | *SO-no*   (sono) |
| American | *ah-may-ree-KA-no*   (americano) |
|   Americans | *ah-may-ree-KA-nee*   (americani) |
| and | *ay*   (e) |
| apples | *MAY-lay*   (mele) |
| are | |
|   Are you? | *S‿YAY-tay?*   (Siete?) |
|   They are | *ESS-see SO-no*   (Essi sono) |
|   We are | *S‿YA-mo*   (Siamo) |
| aspirin | *ah-spee-REE-na*   (aspirina) |

**35**

| English | Pronunciation and Italian Spelling |
|---------|-----------------------------------|

## B

| | |
|---|---|
| bad | *kaht-TEE-vo*  (cattivo) |
| bandage | *BEN-da*  (benda) |
| barber | *barb-YAY-ray*  (barbiere) |
| be shaved | |
| I want to be shaved | *day-ZEE-day-ro FAR-mee la BAR-ba* (Desidero farmi la barba) |
| beans | *fa-JO-lee*  (fagioli) |
| bed | *LET-to*  (letto) |
| beef | *MAHN-dzo*  (manzo) |
| beer | *BEER-ra*  (birra) |
| a glass of beer | *oon beek-K⌣YAY-ray dee BEER-ra* (un bicchiere di birra) |
| blankets | *ko-PAYR-tay*  (coperte) |
| boiled water | *AK-kwa bohl-LEE-ta*  (acqua bollita) |
| bottle | *F⌣YA-sko*  (fiasco) |
| a bottle of | *oon F⌣YA-sko dee__*  (un fiasco di__) |
| bread | *PA-nay*  (pane) |
| bridge | *POHN-tay*  (ponte) |
| bring help | *k⌣ya-MA-tay day sohk-KOR-see* (Chiamate dei soccorsi) |

| English | Pronunciation and Italian Spelling |
|---------|-----------------------------------|
| Bring me___ | *por-TA-tay-mee___* (Portatemi___) |
| brush | |
| shaving brush | *pen-NEL-lo payr BAR-ba* (pennello per barba) |
| bus | *A ͜ oo-to-booss* (autobus) |
| butter | *BOOR-ro* (burro) |
| buttons | *boht-TO-nee* (bottoni) |

## C

| | |
|---------|-----------------------------------|
| camp | *KAHM-po* (campo) |
| can | |
| I can | *POHSS-so* (Posso) |
| carrots | *ka-RO-tay* (carote) |
| centesimi | *chen-TAY-zee-mee* (centesimi) |
| chicken | *POHL-lo* (pollo) |
| chocolate | *chohk-ko-LA-ta* (cioccolata) |
| church | *K ͜ YAY-za* (chiesa) |
| cigarettes | *see-ga-RET-tay* (sigarette) |
| cigars | *SEE-ga-ree* (sigari) |
| city | *cheet-TA* (città) |

**37**

| English | Pronunciation and Italian Spelling |
|---------|-----------------------------------|
| clothing store | *nay-GOHTS-yo dee ar-TEE-ko-lee da WO-mo* (negozio di articoli da uomo) |
| coffee | *kahf-FAY* (caffe) |
| a cup of coffee | *oo-na TAHT-tsa dee kahf-FAY* (una tazza di caffè) |
| comb | *PET-tee-nay* (pettine) |
| come | *vay-NEE-tay* (venite) |
| Come here | *vay-NEE-tay KWEE* (Venite qui) |
| Come quickly | *vay-NEE-tay PRESS-to* (Venite presto) |
| cost | |
| it costs | *KO-sta* (costa) |
| How much does this cost? | *KWAHN-to KO-sta?* (Quanto costa?) |
| cotton | *ko-TO-nay* (cotone) |
| cover | |
| Take cover! | *MET-tayr-see ahl ree-PA-ro!* (Mettersi al riparo!) |
| cucumbers | *cheet-R_YO-lee* (citrioli) |
| cup | *TAHT-tsa* (tazza) |
| a cup of___ | *oo-na TAHT-tsa dee___* (una tazza di___) |

| English | Pronunciation and Italian Spelling |
|---------|-----------------------------------|

## D

| | |
|---|---|
| Danger! | *pay-REE-ko-lo!* (Pericolo!) |
| day | *JOR-no* (giorno) |
| Good day | *bwohn JOR-no* (Buon giorno) |
| dentist | *den-TEE-sta* (dentista) |
| disinfectant | *dee-zeen-fet-TAHN-tay* (disinfettante) |
| Do you understand? | *ah-VAY-tay ka-PEE-to?* (Avete capito?) |
| doctor | *MAY-dee-ko* (medico) |
| Take me to a doctor | *ahk-kohm-pahn-YA-tay-mee da oon MAY-dee-ko* (Accompagnatemi da un medico) |
| Draw me a map | *FA-tay-mee oo-no SKEET-tso* (Fatemi uno schizzo) |
| drink | *BAY-ray* (bere) |
| drinking water | *AHK-kwa po-TA-bee-lay* (acqua potabile) |
| drugstore | *far-ma-CHEE-ah* (farmacia) |

## E

| | |
|---|---|
| eat | *mahn-JA-ray* (mangiare) |
| eggs | *WO-va* (uova) |
| eight | *OHT-to* (otto) |

| English | Pronunciation and Italian Spelling |
|---|---|
| eighteen | *dee-CHOHT-to* (diciotto) |
| eighty | *oht-TAHN-ta* (ottanta) |
| eleven | *OON-dee-chee* (undici) |
| evening | *SAY-ra* (sera) |
| Good evening | *BWO-na SAY-ra* (Buona sera) |
| Excuse me | *SKOO-za* (scusa) |
| expensive | *KA-ro* (caro) |
| too expensive | *TROHP-po KA-ro* (troppo caro) |

## F

| | |
|---|---|
| far | *lohn-TA-no* (lontano) |
| How far is it? | *ah KAY dee-STAHN-tsa AY?* (A che distanza è?) |
| Is it far? | *AY lohn-TA-no?* (È lontano?) |
| fifteen | *KWEEN-dee-chee* (quindici) |
| fifty | *cheen-KWAHN-ta* (cinquanta) |
| find | *tro-VA-ray* (trovare) |
| Where can I find___? | *DO-vay POHSS-so tro-VA-ray___?* (Dove posso trovare___?) |
| fish | *PAY-shay* (pesce) |

| English | Pronunciation and Italian Spelling |
|---------|-----------------------------------|
| five | *CHEEN-kway* (cinque) |
| food | *da mahn-JA-ray* (da mangiare) |
| fork | *for-KET-ta* (forchetta) |
| forty | *kwa-RAHN-ta* (quaranta) |
| four | *KWAHT-tro* (quattro) |
| fourteen | *kwaht-TOR-dee-chee* (quattordici) |
| Friday | *vay-nayr-DEE* (venerdì) |
| fruit | *FROOT-ta* (frutta) |

## G

| | |
|---|---|
| garage | *ga-RAJ* (garage) |
| Gas! | *GAHSS!* (Gas!) |
| get | |
|   Where can I get___? | *DO-vay POHSS-so tro-VA-ray___?* (Dove posso trovare___?) |
| Give me___ | *DA-tay-mee___* (Datemi___) |
| glass | *beek-K⌣YAY-ray* (bicchiere) |
|   a glass of___ | *oon beek-K⌣YAY-ray dee___* (un bicchiere di___) |
| go | *ahn-DA-tay!* (Andate!) |
|   Go quickly | *ahn-DA-tay PRESS-to!* (Andate presto!) |

| English | Pronunciation and Italian Spelling |
|---------|-------------------------------------|
| good | *BWO-no* (buono) |
| Good day | *bwohn JOR-no* (Buon giorno) |
| Good evening | *BWO-na SAY-ra* (Buona sera) |
| Good luck | *BWO-na for-TOO-na* (Buona fortuna) |
| Good morning | *bwohn JOR-no* (Buon giorno) |
| Good-by | *ar-ree-vay-DAYR-chee* (Arrivederci) |
| grapes | *OO-va* (uva) |
| grocery | *nay-GOHTS-yo dee JAY-nay-ree ah-lee-men-TA-ree* (negozio di generi alimentari) |

## H

| hair | *ka-PEL-lee* (capelli) |
|------|--------------------------|
| have my hair cut | *FAR-mee tahl-YA-ray ee ka-PEL-lee* (farmi tagliare i capelli) |
| half | |
| half past six | *lay SAY ay MED-dza* (le sei e mezza) |
| Halt! | *AHL-to LA!* (Alto là!) |
| ham | *pro-SHOOT-to* (prosciutto) |
| handkerchief | *faht-tso-LET-to* (fazzoletto) |

| English | Pronunciation and Italian Spelling |
|---|---|
| have | |
| Have you? | *ah-VAY-tay?* (Avete?) |
| I have | *O* (Ho) |
| I don't have | *nohn O* (Non ho) |
| We have | *ahb-B‿YA-mo* (Abbiamo) |
| We don't have | *nohn ahb-B‿YA-mo* (Non abbiamo) |
| have my clothes washed | *FAR la-VA-ray del-la b‿yahn-kay-REE-ah* (far lavare della biancheria) |
| have my hair cut | *FAR-mee tahl-YA-ray ee ka-PEL-lee* (farmi tagliare i capelli) |
| he | *EL-yee* (egli) |
| he is | *EL-yee AY* (Egli è) |
| Help! | *ah-YOO-to!* (Aiuto!) |
| Bring help | *k‿ya-MA-tay day sohk-KOR-see* (Chiamate dei soccorsi) |
| Help me | *ah-yoo-TA-tay-mee* (Aiutatemi) |
| here | *KWEE* (quì) |
| highway | *a‿oo-to-STRA-da* (autostrada) |
| hospital | *o-spay-DA-lay* (ospedale) |
| Take me to the hospital | *ahk-kohm-pahn-YA-tay-mee ahl-lo-spay-DA-lay* (Accompagnatemi all'ospedale) |

| English | Pronunciation and Italian Spelling |
|---------|-----------------------------------|
| hot water | *AHK-kwa KAHL-da*  (acqua calda) |
| hotel | *o-TEL*  (hotel) |
| Where is a hotel? | *do-VAY lo-TEL?*  (Dov'è l'hotel?) |
| house | *KA-za*  (casa) |
| how | *KO-may*  (come) |
| How do you say___? | *KO-may see K⌣YA-ma___?*  (Come si chiama___?) |
| *or* | *KO-may see DEE-chay___?*  (Come si dice___?) |
| How far is it? | *ah KAY dee-STAHN-tsa AY?*  (A che distanza è?) |
| How much | *KWAHN-to*  (quanto) |
| How much does this cost? | *KWAHN-to KO-sta?*  (Quanto costa?) |
| hundred | *CHEN-to*  (cento) |
| hungry | |
| I am hungry | *O FA-may*  (Ho fame) |

**I**

| | |
|---|---|
| I | *EE⌣o*  (io) |
| I am | *SO-no*  (sono) |

| English | Pronunciation and Italian Spelling |
|---|---|
| I have | *O* (ho) |
| I don't have | *nohn O* (Non ho) |
| I want | *day-ZEE-day-ro* (desidero) |
| *or* | *VOHL-yo* (voglio) |
| ice cream | *jay-LA-to* (gelato) |
| in Italian | *een ee-tahl-YA-no* (in italiano) |
| ink | *eenk-YO-stro* (inchiostro) |
| iodine | *teen-TOO-ra DOHD-yo* (tintura d'odio) |
| is | *AY* (è) |
| He is | *EL-yee AY* (Egli è) |
| It is | *AY* (è) |
| It is not | *nohn AY* (Non è) |
| Is it far? | *AY lohn-TA-no?* (È lontano?) |
| What is it? | *ko-ZAY* (Cos'è?) |
| Where is it? | *do-VAY?* (Dov'è?) |
| Where is there___? | *DO-vay CHAY___?* (Dove c'è___?) |
| Italian | *ee-tahl-YA-no* (italiano) |
| in Italian | *een ee-tahl-YA-no* (in italiano) |

## K

| | |
|---|---|
| kilometers | *kee-LO-may-tree* (chilometri) |
| knife | *kohl-TEL-lo* (coltello) |

| English | Pronunciation and Italian Spelling |
|---------|-----------------------------------|

### L

| | |
|---|---|
| lamb | *ahn-YEL-lo* (agnello) |
| laxative | *lahss-sa-TEE-vo* (lassativo) |
| leave | |
|   it leaves | *PAR-tay* (parte) |
| left | |
|   Turn left | *JEE-ra ah see-NEE-stra* (Gira a sinistra) |
| lemon | *lee-MO-nay* (limone) |
| lire | *LEE-ray* (lire) |
| lost | *spayr-DOO-to* (sperduto) |
|     *or* | *spayr-DOO-tee* (sperduti) |
| luck | *for-TOO-na* (fortuna) |
|   Good luck | *BWO-na for-TOO-na* (Buona fortuna) |

### M

| | |
|---|---|
| madam | *seen-YO-ra* (signora) |
| main street | *STRA-da preen-chee-PA-lay* (strada principale) |
| map | *SKEET-tso* (schizzo) |
|   Draw me a map | *FA-tay-mee oo-no SKEET-tso* (Fatemi uno schizzo) |
| market | *mayr-KA-to* (mercato) |

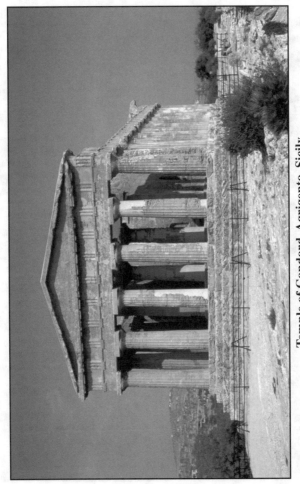

Temple of Condord, Agrigento, Sicily

**Duomo, Tuscany**

| English | Pronunciation and Italian Spelling |
|---------|-----------------------------------|
| matches | *f‿yahm-MEE-fay-ree* (fiammiferi) |
| mattress | *ma-tay-RAHSS-so* (materasso) |
| me | *mee* (mi) |
| meat | *KAR-nay* (carne) |
| mechanic | *mek-KA-nee-ko* (meccanico) |
| milk | *LAHT-tay* (latte) |
| minus | *MAY-no* (meno) |
| minute | *mee-NOO-to* (minuto) |
| Wait a minute! | *ah-spet-TA-tay oon mee-NOO-to!* (Aspettate un minuto!) |
| miss | *seen-yo-REE-na* (signorina) |
| mister | *seen-YO-ray* (signore) |
| Monday | *loo-nay-DEE* (lunedì) |
| mosquito net | *dzahn-dzar-YAY-ra* (zanzariera) |
| movie | *FEELM* (film) |
| When does the movie start? | *ah KAY O-ra ko-MEEN-cha eel FEELM?* (A che ora comincia il film?) |

## N

| name | |
|------|--|
| My name is__ | *EE‿o mee K‿YA-mo___* (Io mi chiamo__) |

| English | Pronunciation and Italian Spelling |
|---|---|
| What is your name? | KO-may see K‿YA-ma? (Come si chiama?) |
| near | vee-CHEE-no (vicino) |
| the nearest town | eel pa-AY-zay P‿YOO vee-CHEE-no (il paese più vicino) |
| needle | AH-go (ago) |
| nine | NO-vay (nove) |
| nineteen | dee-chahn-NO-vay (diciannove) |
| ninety | no-VAHN-ta (novanta) |
| no | NO (no) |
| north | NORD (nord) |
| Which way is north? | do-VAY eel NORD? (Dov'e il nord?) |
| not | NOHN (non) |

## O

| | |
|---|---|
| of | dee (di) |
| a bottle of wine | oon F‿YA-sko dee VEE-no (un fiasco di vino) |
| a cup of coffee | oo-na TAHT-tsa dee kahf-FAY (una tazza di caffè) |
| a cup of tea | oo-na TAHT-tsa dee TAY (una tazza di tè) |
| a glass of beer | oon beek-K‿YAY-ray dee BEER-ra (un bicchiere di birra) |

| English | Pronunciation and Italian Spelling |
|---------|-----------------------------------|
| **quarter of eight** | *lay OHT-to MAY-no oon KWAR-to* (le otto meno un quarto) |
| *or* | *oon KWAR-to AHL-lay OHT-to* (un quarto alle otto) |
| **one** | *OO-no* (uno) |
| **onions** | *chee-POHL-lay* (cipolle) |
| **orange** | *ah-RAHN-cha* (arancia) |

## P

**past**

| | |
|---|---|
| **half past six** | *lay SAY ay MED-dza* (le sei e mezza) |
| **quarter past five** | *lay CHEEN-kway ay oon KWAR-to* (le cinque e un quarto) |
| **ten past two** | *lay DOO-ay ay D‿YAY-chee* (le due e dieci) |

**pay**

| | |
|---|---|
| **I will pay you** | *VEE pa-gay-RO* (Vi pagherò) |
| **peas** | *pee-ZEL-lee* (piselli) |
| **pen** | *PEN-na* (penna) |
| **pencil** | *ma-TEE-ta* (matita) |
| **pepper** | *PAY-pay* (pepe) |
| **pillow** | *koo-SHEE-no* (cuscino) |

| English | Pronunciation and Italian Spelling |
|---------|-----------------------------------|
| pins | *SPEEL-lee*  (spilli) |
| safety pins | *SPEEL-lee dee see-koo-RET-tsa*  (spilli di sicurezza) |
| pipe | *PEE-pa*  (pipa) |
| pipe tobacco | *ta-BAHK-ko payr PEE-pa*  (tabacco per pipa) |
| plate | *P⏝YAHT-to*  (piatto) |
| please | *payr fa-VO-ray*  (per favore) |
| or | *payr p⏝ya-CHAY-ray*  (per piacere) |
| point |  |
| Point it out to me | *een-dee-KA-tay-mee*  (Indicatemi) |
| police station | *kwess-TOO-ra*  (questura) |
| policeman | *GWARD-ya*  (guardia) |
| pork | *ma-YA-lay*  (maiale) |
| porter | *fahk-KEE-no*  (facchino) |
| post office | *oof-FEE-cho po-STA-lay*  (ufficio postale) |
| potatoes | *pa-TA-tay*  (patate) |

## Q

| | |
|---|---|
| quarter | *KWAR-to*  (quarto) |
| quarter of eight | *lay OHT-to MAY-no oon KWAR-to*  (le otto meno un quarto) |
| or | *oon KWAR-to AHL-lay OHT-to*  (un quarto alle otto) |

| English | Pronunciation and Italian Spelling |
|---|---|
| quarter past five | *lay CHEEN-kway ay oon KWAR-to* <br> (le cinque e un quarto) |
| quickly | *PRESS-to* (presto) |
| Come quickly! | *vay-NEE-tay PRESS-to!* (Venite presto!) |
| Go quickly! | *ahn-DA-tay PRESS-to!* (Andate presto!) |

## R

| | |
|---|---|
| railroad | *fayr-ro-VEE-ah* (ferrovia) |
| railroad station | *stahts-YO-nay* (stazione) |
| rain coat | *eem-payr-may-AH-bee-lay* (impermeabile) |
| razor | *ra-ZO-yo* (rasoio) |
| razor blades | *LA-may da ra-ZO-yo* (lame da rasoio) |
| rest | *ree-po-ZA-ray* (riposare) |
| restaurant | *ress-to-RAHN* (restaurant) |
| *or* | *ree-sto-RAHN-tay* (ristorante) |
| Where is the restaurant? | *do-VAY eel ress-to-RAHN?* (Dov'è il restaurant?) |
| rice | *REE-zo* (riso) |

| English | Pronunciation and Italian Spelling |
|---------|-----------------------------------|
| right | |
|   Turn right | *JEE-ra ah DESS-tra*   (Gira a destra) |
| right away | *PRESS-to*   (presto) |
| river | *F‿YOO-may*   (fiume) |
| road | *STRA-da*   (strada) |
| room | *KA-may-ra*   (camera) |

## S

| English | Pronunciation and Italian Spelling |
|---------|-----------------------------------|
| safety pins | *SPEEL-lee dee see-koo-RET-tsa*   (spilli di sicurezza) |
| salad | *een-sa-LA-ta*   (insalata) |
| salt | *SA-lay*   (sale) |
| Saturday | *SA-ba-to*   (sabato) |
| say | |
|   How do you say___? | *KO-may see K‿YA-ma___?*   (Come si chiama___?) |
|     *or* | *KO-may see DEE-chay___?*   (Come si dice___?) |
| servant | *oon ka-mayr-YAY-ray*   (un cameriere) |
| seven | *SET-tay*   (sette) |
| seventeen | *dee-chass-SET-tay*   (diciassette) |
| seventy | *set-TAHN-ta*   (settanta) |

**52**

| English | Pronunciation and Italian Spelling |
|---------|-----------------------------------|
| shave | |
|   I want to be shaved | *day-ZEE-day-ro FAR-mee la BAR-ba* (Desidero farmi la barba) |
|   shaving brush | *pen-NEL-lo payr BAR-ba* (pennello payr barba) |
|   shaving soap | *sa-PO-nay payr BAR-ba* (sapone per barba) |
| she | *ESS-sa* (essa) |
| sheets | *lent-SWO-la* (lenzuola) |
| shirt | *ka-MEE-cha* (camicia) |
| shoes | *SKAR-pay* (scarpe) |
|   shoe laces | *LAHT-chee da SKAR-pay* (lacci da scarpe) |
|   shoe polish | *CHAY-ra payr SKAR-pay* (cera per scarpe) |
|   shoemaker | *kahl-tso-LA-yo* (calzolaio) |
| sick | *ahm-ma-LA-to* (ammalato) |
|       *or* | *ahm-ma-LA-tee* (ammalati) |
| sir | *seen-YO-ray* (signore) |
| six | *SAY* (sei) |
| sixteen | *SAY-dee-chee* (sedici) |
| sixty | *sess-SAHN-ta* (sessanta) |
| sleep | *dor-MEE-ray* (dormire) |
| slowly | *ah-DA-jo* (adagio) |
| soap | *sa-PO-nay* (sapone) |

| English | Pronunciation and Italian Spelling |
|---|---|
| soldiers | *sohl-DA-tee* (soldati) |
| soup | *mee-NESS-tra* (minestra) |
| speak | *par-LA-tay* (parlate) |
| Speak slowly | *par-LA-tay ah-DA-jo* (Parlate adagio) |
| spinach | *spee-NA-chee* (spinaci) |
| spoon | *kook-K⌣YA-yo* (cucchiaio) |
| spring | *sor-JEN-tay* (sorgente) |
| start | |
| it starts | *ko-MEEN-cha* (comincia) |
| When does the movie start? | *ah KAY O-ra ko-MEEN-cha eel FEELM?* (A che ora comincia il film?) |
| station | *stahts-YO-nay* (stazione) |
| Where is the railroad station? | *do-VAY la stahts-YO-nay?* (Dov'è la stazione?) |
| steak | *bee-STEK-ka* (bistecca) |
| Stop! | *fayr-MA-tay-vee!* (Fermatevi!) |
| straight ahead | *dee-REET-to* (diritto) |
| street | *STRA-da* (strada) |
| main street | *STRA-da preen-chee-PA-lay* (strada principale) |
| sugar | *TSOOK-kay-ro* (zucchero) |
| Sunday | *do-MAY-nee-ka* (domenica) |

**54**

**Florence**

**Square, Radda**

| English | Pronunciation and Italian Spelling |
|---------|-----------------------------------|

### T

| | |
|---|---|
| tailor | *SAR-to*   (sarto) |
| take | |
| take a bath | *PREN-day-ray oon BAHN-yo*   (prendere un bagno) |
| Take cover! | *MET-tayr-see ahl ree-PA-ro!*   (Mettersi al riparo!) |
| Take me there | *ahk-kohm-pahn-YA-tay-mee LA*   (Accompagnatemi là) |
| Take me to a doctor | *ahk-kohm-pahn-YA-tay-mee da oon MAY-dee-ko*   (Accompagnatemi da un medico) |
| Take me to the hospital | *ahk-kohm-pahn-YA-tay-mee ahl-lo-spay-DA-lay*   (Accompagnatemi all'ospedale) |
| tea | *TAY*   (tè) |
| a cup of tea | *oo-na TAHT-tsa dee TAY*   (una tazza di tè) |
| telegraph office | *loof-FEE-cho tay-lay-GRA-fee-ko*   (l'ufficio telegrafico) |
| telephone | *tay-LAY-fo-no*   (telefono) |
| ten | *D‿YAY-chee*   (dieci) |
| thank you | *GRAHTS-yay*   (grazie) |
| the | *eel*   (il) |
| *or* | *la*   (la) |
| *or* | *ee*   (i) |

**55**

| English | Pronunciation and Italian Spelling |
|---|---|
| there | *LA* (là) |
| Take me there | *ahk-kohm-pahn-YA-tay-mee LA* (Accompagnatemi là) |
| they | *ESS-see* (essi) |
| thirsty | |
| I am thirsty | *O SAY-tay* (Ho sete) |
| thirteen | *TRAY-dee-chee* (tredici) |
| thirty | *TREN-ta* (trenta) |
| thirty-one | *tren-TOO-no* (trentuno) |
| thirty-two | *tren-ta-DOO-ay* (trentadue) |
| this | *KWESS-to* (questo) |
| What's this? | *ko-ZAY KWESS-to?* (Cos'è questo?) |
| thousand | *MEEL-lay* (mille) |
| thread | *FEE-lo* (filo) |
| three | *TRAY* (tre) |
| Thursday | *jo-vay-DEE* (giovedì) |
| time | |
| At what time? | *ah KAY O-ra?* (A che ora?) |
| What time is it? | *kay O-ra AY?* (Che ora è?) |

| English | Pronunciation and Italian Spelling |
|---|---|
| tired | *STAHN-ko* (stanco) |
| or | *STAHN-kee* (stanchi) |
| to | |
| to a doctor | *da oon MAY-dee-ko* (da un medico) |
| to a hospital | *ahl-lo-spay-DA-lay* (all'ospedale) |
| three minutes to nine | *lay NO-vay MAY-no TRAY* (le nove meno tre) |
| tobacco | *ta-BAHK-ko* (tabacco) |
| pipe tobacco | *ta-BAHK-ko payr PEE-pa* (tabacco per pipa) |
| today | *OHD-jee* (oggi) |
| toilet | *ga-bee-NET-to* (gabinetto) |
| Where is a toilet? | *do-VAY eel ga-bee-NET-to?* (Dov'è il gabinetto?) |
| tomato | *po-mo-DO-ro* (pomodoro) |
| tomorrow | *do-MA-nee* (domani) |
| too expensive | *TROHP-po KA-ro* (troppo caro) |
| tooth paste | *PA-sta den-tee-FREE-cha* (pasta dentifricia) |
| toothbrush | *spaht-tso-LEE-no da DEN-tee* (spazzolino di denti) |
| towel | *ah-shoo-ga-MA-no* (asciugamano) |
| town | *pa-AY-zay* (paese) |

| English | Pronunciation and Italian Spelling |
|---|---|
| the nearest town | *eel pa-AY-zay P‿YOO vee-CHEE-no* (il paese più vicino) |
| train | *TRAY-no* (treno) |
| When does the train leave? | *ah KAY O-ra PAR-tay eel TRAY-no?* (A che ora parte il treno?) |
| Tuesday | *mar-tay-DEE* (martedì) |
| Turn! | *JEE-ra!* (Gira!) |
| Turn left | *JEE-ra ah see-NEE-stra* (Gira a sinistra) |
| Turn right | *JEE-ra ah DESS-tra* (Gira a destra) |
| twelve | *DO-dee-chee* (dodici) |
| twenty | *VEN-tee* (venti) |
| twenty-one | *ven-TOO-no* (ventuno) |
| twenty-two | *ven-tee-DOO-ay* (ventidue) |
| two | *DOO-ay* (due) |
| two o'clock | *SO-no lay DOO-ay* (Sono le due) |

## U

| | |
|---|---|
| undershirt | *MAHL-ya* (maglia) |
| undershorts | *moo-TAHN-day* (mutande) |
| understand | |
| Do you understand? | *ah-VAY-tay ka-PEE-to?* (Avete capito?) |
| I don't understand | *NOHN ka-PEE-sko* (Non capisco) |

## V

| veal | *vee-TEL-lo* (vitello) |
| vegetables | *vayr-DOO-ra* (verdura) |
| *or* | *lay-GOO-mee* (legumi) |

## W

| Wait a minute! | *ah-spet-TA-tay oon mee-NOO-to!* |
| | (Aspettate un minuto!) |

**want**

| I want__ *or*<br>I want<br>to__ | *day-ZEE-day-ro__* (desidero__) |
| *or* | *VOHL-yo__* (voglio__) |
| We want__ | *day-zee-dayr-YA-mo* (desideriamo) |

**wash up**

| I want to<br>wash up | *day-ZEE-day-ro la-VAR-mee* (Desidero<br>lavarmi) |
| Watch out! | *aht-tents-YO-nay!* (Attenzione!) |
| water | *AHK-kwa* (acqua) |
| boiled water | *AHK-kwa bohl-LEE-ta* (acqua bollita) |
| drinking<br>water | *AHK-kwa po-TA-bee-lay* (acqua potabile) |
| hot water | *AHK-kwa KAHL-da* (acqua calda) |

**59**

| English | Pronunciation and Italian Spelling |
|---------|-----------------------------------|
| we | |
| We are | S‿YA-mo  (Siamo) |
| We have | abh-B‿YA-mo  (Abbiamo) |
| We don't have | nohn ahb-B‿YA-mo  (Non abbiamo) |
| We want__ | day-zee-dayr-YA-mo__ (Desideriamo__) |
| Wednesday | mayr-ko-lay-DEE  (mercoledì) |
| well (for water) | POHT-tso  (pozzo) |
| well | BAY-nay  (bene) |
| I am well | STO BAY-nay  (Sto bene) |
| what | KO-za  (cosa) |
| At what time | ah KAY O-ra  (A che ora?) |
| What is this? | ko-ZAY KWESS-to?  (Cos'è questo?) |
| What is your name? | KO-may see K‿YA-ma?  (Come si chiama?) |
| What time is it? | kay O-ra AY?  (Che ora è?) |
| when | |
| When does the movie start? | ah KAY O-ra ko-MEEN-cha eel FEELM? (A che ora comincia il film?) |
| When does the train leave? | ah KAY O-ra PAR-tay eel TRAY-no? (A che ora parte il treno?) |

60

| English | Pronunciation and Italian Spelling |
|---|---|
| where | *DO-vay* (dove) |
| Where are they? | *DO-vay SO-no?* (Dove sono?) |
| Where is it? | *do-VA Y?* (Dov'è?) |
| Where is there___? | *DO-vay CHA Y___?* (Dove c'è___?) |
| Where can I find *or* get___? | *DO-vay POHSS-so tro-VA-ray___?* (Dove posso trovare___?) |
| which | *KWA-lay* (quale) |
| Which is the road to___? | *kwa-LA Y la STRA-da payr___?* (Qual'è la strada per___?) |
| Which way is north? | *do-VA Y eel NORD?* (Dov'è il nord?) |
| wine | *VEE-no* (vino) |
| a bottle of wine | *oon F⌣YA-sko dee VEE-no* (un fiasco di vino) |
| workman | *o-pay-RA-yo* (operaio) |
| wounded | *fay-REE-to* (ferito) |
| *or* | *fay-REE-tee* (feriti) |

# Y

| | |
|---|---|
| yes | *SEE* (sì) |
| yesterday | *YA Y-ree* (ieri) |
| you | *VO Y* (voi) |
| Are you? | *S⌣YA Y-tay?* (Siete?) |
| Have you? | *ah-VA Y-tay?* (Avete?) |
| I will pay you | *vee pa-gay-RO* (Vi pagherò) |

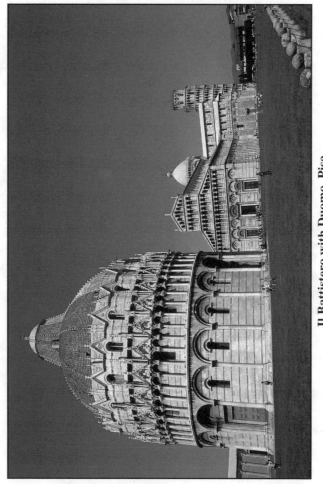

Il Battistero with Duomo, Pisa